pieces

pieces

volume ONE

For anyone who ever felt like their heart was in pieces or lost someone who captured their soul. For anyone trying to find balance in the midst of chaos. For anyone willing to get lost within these pages.

*Come and take
this journey with me*

Here
lies
pieces
of
me

Table of Contents

Energy:
"You are within me. I am within you. We are one".
We are all linked through our etheric connection
which allows us to raise our frequency and vibration.

Mind and Body:
"Without the mind, the body cannot exist.
Without the body, there is no keeper for the mind".
Here you will discover my pains, passions, and truths all
hidden within the infinite space and dimensions of the mind.

Heart:
"The giver of life, the breaker of souls".
You will explore the ups and downs, as well
as the highs and lows of this beautiful vessel.

Soul:
"The portal within us all".
Here you will explore the infinite
light and darkness of the soul.

Without the mind, the body cannot exist. Without the body there is no keeper for the mind

mind & body

I remember the day
we laid in your bed

and I told you how
hard it would be to love me

I wish you would've
listened

-then maybe we would still be friends

So many of our words become lost in our inability to demolish our walls and reveal our truths

I cannot hide who I am and I cannot clothe
what I feel

-unmasked

Is it wrong
to build a cocoon
so that I may
blossom into a
butterfly?

All I have left of you is memories that
constantly play over and over in my head.
Like a mirage, I see you each day, thinking I
can touch you. Reaching out to find, it is all
in my mind

Still,

traces of you
can be found
within the jumbled
components of my brain

HUNGER

There's this hunger within me

My soul rumbling and aching to make it

Itching to be free of poverty and broken
dreams

Dying to manifest day dreams into realities

Living to bring life to everything that I feign

With each breath this hunger digging deeper
into my spleen

This voice yelling inside of me,
saying,

> *I gotta make it*

Through all the pain,

I smile.
I conquer.
I succeed.

With you,
I can't show emotion
I gotta' play it cool
And wait to text you back
In two days
Maybe a few
Just to show you my light
Show you I'm beautiful
And keep my feelings on a chain
Never releasing them to you

A Woman's Purpose

Will anybody ever love me? And is my life defined by the man who does? Why does it seem like a woman's life is confined to this shaggy box of finding love? Does a man make me who I am or molds me into who I need to be? Cause I thought being a woman was me embodying everything within me...

More or Less.

You felt like keeping me out of your circle was what was best. More or less I lost respect. More or less I keep it pushing so I'm free of stress. So I'm free of regret. So the best version of me could manifest. Things just kept going left. Think I'll always love you but that energy will remain locked in my chest. Felt like our love was a test I could never pass. More or less, if I continued chasing you I would've never outgrown my past. Wish things could've last, but how you switched up showed me that the best option was to get gone and press the gas. More or less. Now I progress. Now I soar. I rise. I conquer my goals and focus on what's next.

More or less,
I lost you
and got closer to success.

Phone Home

There are times when I hurt so bad it's as if my wounds would bleed tears. And moments when I'm in shambles but I pretend as if I hold no fear. Even times when I feel so alone that I want to run away. But there's not a dollar to my name and no place to escape. If I had a spaceship and an ample amount of time. I would search the galaxy for a place that I could call mine. A place to ease my mind, ease the pain and erase the times. The moments I ever felt the urge to cry if not for happiness. A place where I was wiped of pain and surrounded by bliss. And if this place exists, I pray the aliens come and rescue me. To bring me to my true home in a different galaxy. In a different world where I can be me and being me is alright. And where I wouldn't have to worry about making it tonight. I know it's out there and maybe one day I'll go. But until then, I cry and weep but never give up hope.

Magic Treehouse

When you and I lock lips and intertwine hips, I become transformed. Feeling high and free off your magic tree, sprouting so gracefully beneath me that I water it with my sacred juices, so effortlessly. Filling my garden with your seeds, planting pieces of you into my roots and... we create rain then waterfalls while tremors of joy spill from our lips. Flowing with the wind, feeling passionately exalted. Feeling as if the universe has aligned, hoping this isn't a lie, asking myself: am I in love?

You reminded me why
life was beautiful

Over-Thinking

I forgot the simple things. I forgot to laugh, smile, and care. Instead I became trampled with thoughts and became lost in them

May I be strong enough to realize and understand that I do not need to control anything but my actions and I need not worry about anything outside of my control

-May I?

How could someone who said they loved you, leave so easily. Like we did not exist. Like we didn't share all of our fears and secrets. Like we were strangers reciting meaningless dialogue, yet we made it look so real.

I wonder if
you still think
about me when
you are with them...

For many faces
have looked
their eyes
into mine
and said they
would always
be there

-but they never stayed

Many times I've made a fool out of myself,
chasing after men who didn't deserve me,
yet filled voids within me that I couldn't
face

Piece
by
piece,
I unravel,
I unfold.
Wishing some pieces weren't broken.
Wishing some pieces could be molded.

You helped me forget that I was trampled with burdens that existed before my existence. You peeled off the illusion that I was chained and helped me discover that I've always been free.

And that's
how I feel,
Just like
the sun,

I don't give
a damn
about the clouds
trying to block me,

I am
still going
to shine

Can I unpeel pieces of your mind? Much rather see what lies inside, though what you hold between your thighs is appealing. I want to bring you healing. Though you're my sexual stimulant, it's your intellect that I'm feeling. Concealing my feelings, I love your body, but our love is more revealing.

You make me want to write poetry
and poetically describe what you are to me
How your presence rises my frequency
and how I feel the peace in your energy
How you fill my plate with love and fuck
me mentally

Pleasing me with your beautiful thoughts,
getting lost in the vibe

I can't see what you see
So I break you trying to run from me
And the pieces of me that I despise
Living a lie
Losing my mind
Slipping through time
Can anybody help me?
Cause'…
You love me
But I'm too below to see
And I know I may lose you
Trying to erase me
And though you higher my frequency
I'm drowned by my demons that speak

some days
I can't imagine
life without you,
others I am bombarded
by the hurt
knowing I must leave now
in order to make
this work
yet your last words
sunk me deeper
than the earth
and cut so deep,

how could I ever return?

Happiest Wishes

On days I should be the happiest, I lie around
dazed and confused
Wondering why my happiest moments are
not spent with you
Knowing we should go our separate ways
after all we've been through
But still I lie around with a plastered smile
wishing I was with you

Conversation?

Not wanting to fall
victim to my emotions
Not wanting to lose
my head
But my head is full
of shit I couldn't say
because you left me
tongue tied and speechless.
Unable to reveal
my truths
Words spilling out
of my ears rather
than resonating within
The need to be heard
rummaging through me,

Demanding a conversation.

You are in every memory
Even the ones before you became mine
You have always been and will forever be
The one who has my heart and breaks it
every time

I spent my days
lost in confusion
Lost in the wind
Stuck in my mind
Stuck in what ifs

I no longer need
your opinions
to define my destiny.
For I have
created my own.

We spend eternity trying to fit into the box
they've created. But I will spend the rest of
my eons trying to break free

-I will never fit into a box

You brightened
my days by
a billion times

I felt you beyond what you're used to. Beyond the flesh and free tree's you possess. Or your Toyota that felt like a jet.

Cause' we vibed

And got high off the energy that you and I provide. Getting lifted from our own telepathic supplies. Yet things always go left, can't blame neither you nor I. We're just butterflies. And with time, I know my worries constantly brought you stress. Yet I pressed and pressed cause my mind was a wreck. I guess it was time to press eject. Cause' what is love if not a paradise? Trying to love you while I'm scared out my mind. With a wall ten feet tall and still three more to climb.

Usually I'd be quick to walk away,
because *you* so easily pushed *me* away. But I've learned to play it cool and take it day by day. Watching you love and engage your time with women who could never surpass what we've created. But I won't stand jealous or in your way. And I won't kick you to the curb or bash your name. I'll let you live and simply find your way. Not saying that when your mind changes I'll be here to stay. Cause' hunny, I don't plan to wait. And every time I did that my days simply went to waste.

So,

Now a days I'm just letting anyone fill your space. Still whether my eyes are opened or closed all I see is your face. And most days I wish these memories would erase. But I know that life works at its own pace. And even though our roads might not ever meet or run the same. Somehow I'm still hoping this beautiful energy remains.

4 UR EYEZ

I am not perfect. I have made countless, countless mistakes. I have done and said things that I am not proud of. I have felt ashamed, depressed, and worthless. But I hold within me a power, a gift, a purpose. And no matter how many times I mess up, I feel ashamed, embarrassed, or worthless, I will never ever give up on myself.

i've always wanted
to be an actress
yet this is the hardest thing
i've ever had to pretend
and acting like I
don't love you
is truly killing me
within

Part of me is quick to erase you, the other part of me sways. My indecisiveness is probably the reason you walked away. But why should you stay locked in my head? I want for you to leave. After all my pain and grief... Not sure if you're worth it honestly. Cause' maybe I never knew you and you never knew me. And maybe we're just not meant to be. Maybe I don't deserve you and don't deserve me.

-Maybe

In silence I mask my pain. Letting the silence speak volumes. Letting it cover my shame. Letting it make you believe I am strong when truly I am going insane.

I can't decipher if you were real or fake. Just trying to keep my head up knowing all the shit I've faced. Feeling like no one can take your place. And I swallow that thought as I watch you willing let another fill my space.

Slowly, surely
You become a stranger
You become a distant memory and someday
I won't know you at all

-eternal sunshine

Dear Self,

This is your life. Stop living for other people.

Peace is a mindset. Happiness is a mindset. Freedom is a mindset. Anything that you want to achieve starts with the mind.

how my eyes cry in despise to think that you
will never know what it's like
to be twenty-four or twenty-five
to be anything other than who you were
before you died

-since you've been gone

Still I Cry...
Inspired by Tupac Shakur

They say they love me,
but still I cry
Only the source of my tears
can dry my eyes
Things getting better now,
but still I cry
A river or tears slipping,
tearing my insides

You will never die.
You will always live through the
fragmented pieces
of my poetry.

The giver of life,
the breaker of souls

heart

I know how this

ends every time,

but I still

invite you

in

~~Fuck it,~~

You're diving your
way into my heart
and I can't stop it
Breaking down my
walls like you own it
Erasing my pain
with your smile

You always
make everything better

-*conversations with him*

love when you
look at me with
your eyes low
and let them feelings
that you feel slightly show

Dilemmas

You push me to be better and make me
reflect upon myself. You challenge me,
water the roots of my growth, and think of
me in ways that take my breath away. Yet, I
remain guarded and afraid of loving you.

Why am I afraid of being loved?

Dangerously in Love

Dangerously in love with a man who makes my heart jump, my mind calm, and my skin quiver in convulsions. My emotions become impulsive and I lose self-control. I know you know I've been trippin', slightly twisted, within my brain. Would've called Mary Jane, but since her lines been disconnected I can't get her to numb the pain. But who's to blame, Who's ashamed? Is it wrong to admit that I'm afraid? Not playing games, but I know that my mistakes have caused you pain. But if you should know anything, just know that my love is true. Knowing that I assume, pick and choose, and often lose my battles. Yea... I'm a hassle, so slick at the tongue. Constantly telling me you're done, though I'm the one, I cause you hell. Don't want to see us fail, but we're failing while falling too deep. One look in your eyes and I feel weak, can hardly speak at times. So memorized, filled with butterflies, almost hypnotized. I know you feel the energy.

And if after angers peak, we still don't speak, I'll be losing my mind. Hitting your line like, "how can you not talk to me?" Cause after the storm settles and I reach the calm I'm filled with epiphanies. I know you're tired of my apologies. Please pardon me. My love is deep and twisted. Please don't think I'm wicked, I'm just doing my best to love while demons dance on my head. Often, I miscommunicate my words and push you away instead. I know my behavior is often misread, just know that I love you. And every time you're gone, I imagine I touch you. I know you feel what I feel, but dangers in the air. Should I walk away from this or continue loving without a care?

pace yourself,
don't fall too deep
into the web

don't get caught
falling in love,
there's always
danger ahead

I wanted to
love you like
no one has
ever done.
In a way so beautiful,
we would always
remain one.

I wanted to...

Make you feel
alive and brand new.
And be the one
that you would
always choose.

In?

Why is your love so intoxicating? It's like you are the antidote to all my pain. Always soothing my brain though loving you drives me insane. It's like you and I are the same. But the past has me numb, guarded, and feeling ashamed.

You opened up pieces of me that I didn't know I had. Then, leaving as quickly as you came. My heart needing more time to recover. This heart crying and dying to be heard. To be held. But, this mind, these lips and fingertips, smother the cries with silence, never letting my pain be heard.

I wonder when
it stopped
being love

Have this feeling you
feel what I feel in my chest
And we still breathe
the same breathes
And that you
crave me like
I crave you
And your heart
is lone without me
like mine is
without you

I was too afraid to love you. Building walls higher than the skies. Yet, you still pushed, jumped, and climbed your way to love me. To show me. Make me feel you. To prove you cared... And I fell hard into your love, begging never to be free of it.

She had never been in love before. But somehow she'd fallen deep into his mind. Deep into the place where his pineal and soul meet and found herself… caught, tangled, and tied to his thoughts, his spirit, his indigo being.

-*Sunken City*

loving you so deeply
loving you in ways I can't explain
i wish my mind wasn't so afraid
because oddly, seeing your face erases my
pain
and you're the only person that I have ever
craved
yet, my heart is still covered in chains
and my intuition is expecting mistakes
knowing I've let you fully in
still my fear finds its way creeping in.
feeling like I am committing a sin
is it a sin, that I love you?
cause like light set to a forest,
our rage spreads into burning flames
our words like matches setting the fire
ablaze
and, I cry as I watch us burn,
pouring buckets of gasoline with each word
and in the end neither one can accept the
blame
and, just like that forest,
the aftermath lets me know it won't be the
same

The only person I ever truly wanted. The only person I've ever craved, imagined, and laid with. The only person to knock down my cemented walls. Make me fall in love multiple times, take my heart in their hands and see the world differently. The only person to make me so afraid to love because I knew I would fall too deep. Fall all the way open and become weak. The only person to challenge my perspectives and push me to think critically. To make me thirst for life and yearn for future days. The only person to hurt me so bad that I built a wall bigger than the one that crumbled and covered it in chains.

Blue

I know you left with reason. Yet, my heart was set on you. Then you effortlessly shared my love. And now my heart is icy, cold, and blue.

These Days, I'm Tired

The worst of pains.
The worst of me these days. Watching you
live without me. Guess you've found your
wings, you see mine are shattered in dreams.
Of you and I and possibilities. All make
believe. Writing until this pain erase.
Writing until there is nothing left to say,
until I fill all the pages and it gets easier to
escape. How come you don't see me?
Dropping down to my knees wishing things
could somehow be— *easier*. And my heart
wouldn't have to face another dying love.
Another person to realize that they don't
need me and toss me to the side so easily.
These days I question my existence and
wonder if the rest of my days will be full of
sadness and misery. Please send me peace.
Tired of being broken and drained. Tired of
giving when it is not wanted or received.
Tired of loving until my heart faces a
penalty.

Drowning myself
in my words,
They surround me
Trying to fill
the void
of your absence
Trying to calm
the storm
building within me
Knowing nothing can
demolish this
blazing fire
except you
Hearing your voice
Watering my
dying trees
with your presence
Talking it over
Tearing the wall
between us

Dreams& *N I G H T M A R E S*

I can't be focused with you in my front, side, and rear view. The desire to be near you so intense, my mind jumping flips at the thought of you. My heart pounding within your presence, my heart aching when you leave. Caught in what could be instead of what is. I cannot remain your friend for I've fallen too deep to be stably be around you knowing you don't feel me like I feel you. Knowing I've been the cause of all your bad days, aches and pains... feeling my heart ache as I realize I am not the one you need. Yet you will always be the one I dream of.

he said,

if you really care about someone
no matter how much they hurt you
you will still find it in your heart to
listen to their pain and discover
their truths

she said,

I love myself enough to walk away. To work on myself. To create change. To love you from afar rather than to destroy any more of the time and energy we create.

I tried a thousand ways
to show you I love you
and out of those thousand,
none of them worked.

this is the first time in four years that my
Thursday felt empty
felt broken and lacking of energy
you are right where I want to be
and nobody cares that you're missing
no one realizes I've been empty…

cause' no one sees me like you see me
it's like only you looked right in my eyes
and found my soul
and today I wish my eyes could meet yours
so I could tell you what you mean to me
but then I remember we are not speaking
and you have moved on and lost feelings
and all I'm left here to do is to imagine what
if while wishing I was with you

And every time
we fought
my heart bled
in confusion.
Things are never
the same when
it's you I'm losing.

Loving you is uncomfortable
Cause' I don't know if my feelings are safe
And if it's games you choose to play
Or if I'll say something that will have you
screaming in my face
And if that friend you're texting is coming
for my place

Looking at you,

I fall in love
With your melanin
Your mind
Your walk
The critical components of your thoughts
Loving you
Without being taught

I can't stop thinking about what could've been. And what I could've done or said, or changed. But things are so different now. You are not around and we are no longer. Yet this hunger for you burns within me. And oddly I know that when I see you again my brain will become empty. And though currently I am full of things I want to say, when I meet my fate, no words will leave my lips

Maybe you were never who I thought you were. Maybe I never knew who you were at all and you existed simply as the jumbled depiction I painted of you

-"you" (were what my mind created)

Besides,

 I've got trust issues deeper than any ocean. I wish you wouldn't have had me so open. But you had me so open. So open. I couldn't keep my composure. I just wanted to love you. How could I love you? When I was fussing, fighting, and screaming with demons inside of me. So connected to you, I know that you are a part of me. The yin to my yang, we came from the same flame. But maybe things will never be the same. I was never playing games. Were you?

-Flame

You were...

-how I start every poem
about you since we parted ways

I've gave out my number, faked interest, and given time to people just hoping it'd get easier. Just hoping to forget you. Just hoping I could feel something other than this sadness overcoming me because you are not here.

I thought I would
love you forever
Till we were
old and gray
Till my dying day
Till forever and infinity
parted ways...

Our love,
like water
gentle
violent
unpredictable
calming
soothing
my home
my peace
and my fears
beautiful
and breathtaking
grounding
reflective
giver of life
guardian of truth
holder of wisdom

-our love, like water

I wish I hadn't crossed that line and let you inside of my mind. The universe knows how bad I truly wish you were mine. Ever since you and I saw eye to eye, my heart yearns for you to always be mine. But things got destroyed with time and there is no rewind button. I wish I would've stayed your friend and then maybe things wouldn't ever have to end. And you would trust me and I'd trust you and we'd share our infinite thoughts until the moon finds the sun again.

Why am I so blue?

So blue,
loving you

My heart breaking
at the sound
of our vicious
tongues

I know with time I'll get over it. But I don't know how soon. And to be honest I think a part of me will always want you. But you don't feel the same. The arguments and the past made your feelings change. Somehow from your love I can never sway. I realize shit wasn't all great, but it wasn't the worst. I know if we start over we actually have a chance to make this work. But you no longer see my worth.

You are my kryptonite.

The portal within us all

soul

enter my
planet
enter my
zone

i can't speak to you...
i can only speak to you through this poetry

Somehow you bring back old feelings and pull on pieces of my soul… Like you know me… Like you can feel me the same way I feel you… Like I'm all you need… Like we breathe the same breath. Like you have peaked into my brain, found the keys to my love and had no choice but to make me yours…

whether it was a cluster of truths or loosely
spilled lies, either way I will be just fine.

I will still love who you were and who you are, though I may never know who you become

I apologize for all the damage I've done. For all the days I lost myself and demanded you to help replicate the missing pieces that only I could mend.

That Ray Charles

I ain't shit
Other than my thighs,
hips and big lips
I try to show them,
There's more to me
But they rather see,
what lies underneath
Underneath my clothes
Pretending..
Like they see my soul
And though I look whole,
I'm feeling so empty
Cause there's more to me
And I've offered my soul
But they'll only take a peak
If they think it'll get them close to my gold
See no one knows,
who I really am
Other than my complexion, my ass and my
titties
Bet they won't forget
My thighs, my hips,
and pussy lips
As I lie there,

Dying to be free
And when I leave my flesh
I wonder if that's all they'll grieve
Cause' though they're looking at me,
They could never truly see

Some days I write until tears spill down my cheeks, my hand grows tired, and my soul feels empty.

Caught between

love *or* lust

It's hard to trust,

Even o p e n up

These days

i still imagine
you and i
converse
about our
favorite songs,
knowledge,
the universe,
the stars,
while
surrounded
by nature.
l o v e
spreading like
a blazing fire
through our
souls.
your eyes
pouring their secrets
into mine.
my lips falling
into yours
and I sit there
thinking how
i never want this to end

Waiting for the day
I can call you mine
You be all in my mind
So beautiful
But,
You can't see it
Let me free your soul
I know you
Better than they ever will
Let me love you
Let me show you
You want them though
Illusion...
That's all you see
Let me show you,
Real
This love
Will unwind you
Give you love you can't define
Love you can never find
Only with me
O n l y,
Between us

Each day was spent talking for hours, hands intertwined, hearts racing, skin tingling at the slightest touch from one another. Staring into each other's souls

-Sunken city II

You were...

My alien in crime
My extraterrestrial being
My reflection in physical form
The only person to see me in totality

If you understood how beautiful your love
is, you wouldn't be so quick to give it away

-him

He left pieces
of me scattered
across the universe

Your perfections always seem to outweigh your flaws, sinking my teeth deeper into your soul. Tasting your mind, feeling your heart, seeing your love. Branching off connections, strumming my chords, syncing your peace with mine. Loving me. Understanding me. Fighting for me.

I. Love. You. I whisper those words knowing I should shout to signal what you mean to me. But humble I am as I reflect on the joys of your love that quivers my spirit and ignites my flames, fueling me with love. Freeing me of shame. Still I remain quiet when asked how I feel. Watching myself fall into the spell of your energy. Trapping me with your love though here I am free. Sucking, licking, and kissing your way into my being. Almost dreaming when we make love. Like I've fell into outer space and landed on paradise. This is nice. Beyond anything I've ever felt. Forever isn't promised but why would I spend my days with anyone else?

I think I'll always love you. Not because of
our history or because you fill me mentally.
But because inside you are beautiful and
part of you is linked to me.

How hard it is to close the ink filled pages of a book designed to be openly read yet constantly reminded that books are best read when closed

-why you should never be an open book

Value is not found in what you have or who you know, instead it is found within the depths of the awakened soul

Every time we depart my soul won't let you erase. Though I beg it to let you leave, hostage within me you remain. My soul, eyes, and lips scream for you. Yearning you. My mind constantly replaying our escapades. Finally, I come to accept that you will always be alive within me. That our journey ran too deep to ever be washed away.

-Acceptance

Every part

of me

still loves

every piece

of you

I am feeling empty.

Tired of
convincing you.
Tired of
yearning for you.
To love.
To show me
you feel like I do.
Tired of
wanting to know
this is mutual.

Truthfully, every person I let my wall down
for leaves

-*why my walls have chains*

Sometimes I wonder if it was ever real for
you like it was for me

I can feel the
pieces of you and I
that are still connected

08:03

Currently,
I am suffering trying to hollow the tornado
blaring within the pit of my stomach. Trying
to suck in and swallow all that I feel for you.
But, even when the tornado transforms into
quiet splashing waves, the feeling still
remains. I can't break you. I can't release
you from my soul, my spirit, my being. No
matter how hard I try. I bite my tongue, fold
my arms across my chest and fix my lips to
lie to you. To deny you of my soul. To hide
the deepest parts of me that yearn to tell you
all that I feel. How I never want you to
leave. How life just seems so right when are
next to me. How you seem to fit me so
perfectly. How I am in love with your eyes
and your smile. Your locs that hold this
powerful energy. How similar we are
mentally. How we've been crossing paths
way before you slid that note to me.
Still I suffer,
Trying to get you realize this is something
way deeper than you and I could ever
comprehend. Knowing that I have to keep
these feelings held deep within.
Pretending I don't love you.

I look in your eyes
knowing you see
the pieces I hide

Scared out of her mind, yet she loved him. Followed him where colors are free, cement collides, and lost souls reside. Where waves become the music. Where the ocean became one with their souls. Where she knew they could always find each other.

-Sunken City III

Chances

If you gave me the chance
I would love you in a way you couldn't
explain
Love you so deeply I fuck your brain
Love you,
that without me you feel insane
Love you so deeply I could feel every ounce
of your pain

If you let me love you
I promise I'll love you gently
I would explore your soul so deeply
And give you every piece of me
Make you feel every inch of me
Infinitely

And as you pour your love into me,
I'll give you all my energy
Make you feel like you're a king,
Cause you're a god, a beautiful being
A beautiful manifestation of energy
So beautiful,
That I want to love you from the top your
head to the tips of your feet

Let me love you as you are
Let's
open a portal
Where nothing exist but you and me
And when you are down
My love will rise you above your enemies
And float you to a dimension where you are
free
Take all your pain and replace it with loves
high
I'll...
Get you so high
That our souls become intertwined

But currently
I love you from afar
Want to be where you are
Tear down your walls
Free your heart
I'ved…
Loved you from the start
And still,
Things fell apart

But,
If you gave me a chance
I'll love you like you're meant to be
Love you not just physically but mentally
Love you like it's the end of time
My soul wishing you were mine
But the evils got your mind
Telling you I'm make believe
Yet I exist in this reality
If only you would take the chance to see
Knowing you're afraid of being loved
Being loved
Like you're meant to be

Somedays I regret ever letting you get this close to me

I'm sorry I ever told you I loved you. For it was a lie that spilled believably from my lips. Yet I was unable to realize that because I didn't love myself, I had never really loved at all.

-*truths,*
love starts within

I am thankful for the day he left and turned his presence into absence. For this time alone has transformed what was once half into whole.

pieces

and

fragments

of me

are scattered around

your being,

like an aura,

I remain

attached

to your

e n e r g y,

your

frequency,

y o u r

s o u l. . .

calling
and
crying out
to me
while I try
to mend
my own
and
try to
forget
that you and I
ever existed
as one
and how
we've divided ourselves,
placed a line between our beings
and defined ourselves as
strangers
as lovers who once loved
and will love,
no more.

You are within me,
I am within you.
We are one.

energy

For every reason you think you cannot make it, there are many more reasons why you will.

Let your success be louder than their judgments and let your money stack taller than their opinions.

All these people stripped of their wings, yet
trying to tell you how to fly.

-Free yourself

The only person you need to believe in your dream is you.

For all the days you struggled, for all the days you wondered whether you had money in your account, for all the days you wondered how you were going to eat, keep going. Keep preserving. Keep overcoming obstacles. Keep striving.

Practice love.
Without love, life cannot prosper.
Practice peace.
Without peace love will not remain.

Don't let people
tell you your future.
Create your own.

Constantly place effort towards the things you desire so they may manifest not only through faith, but through action

We must first recreate and master the thoughts buried deep in the mind

-where change begins

If you spend all your time worried about
what they are doing, then how will you ever
move forward?

*-the difference between
moving forward and standing still*

The best revenge is doing everything you said you were going to do and them all watching you make it happen.

Don't *ever, ever, eve*r compare yourself to someone else

-note to self

If you don't know
your worth then
who will?

It is important to love yourself. It is important to understand that there is no one else like you and for that reason above you should always love who you are

-reasons to live

You have to look deep inside yourself and find the strength to mend the broken pieces so that you may fly free

Through all the pain you face, all the obstacles you endure, and all the mistakes you have overcame, never give up on yourself

Not everyone will see your vision and that's okay. They don't need to. They'll see it when you get make it happen and succeed even when they said you wouldn't.

Someday you'll look back on these times and appreciate them. You'll be thankful that you never gave up. Because if you had, you'd never know the feeling of finally reaching success.

Whether you choose to acknowledge it or not there are people watching you, looking up to you, depending on you. You are someone's example. Let your life speak.

The worst thing would be to lose something
so beautiful just because you were too afraid
to see it through

Trust your ideas
Follow your dreams
You never
know where they
might take you

How can you truly
appreciate others when
you do not appreciate yourself?

Stop focusing
on the things
you can't control.
Things always work
themselves out.

That thing that you're crying over may or may not come back. It may or may not work out. It may or may not find peace. But life keeps going and you have to keep going as well.

Many times
we are too busy
weaving our own webs
to realize when
someone has been
caught in their own.

Be consistent

-a message from your dreams

They're not stopping for you. So baby girl,
please don't waste time stopping for them.

To love this life is to master strength, happiness, peace, and self-discipline. To be free of others judgments and opinions. To live only for who you are and strive to be.

You can have it all,
But if you try to do it all
Without first mastering one
You will never accomplish anything

-wise words from my mother

You have to look deep inside yourself and find the strength to mend the broken pieces so that you may fly free

Strength is found
in the woman
bold enough
to be herself

Sometimes you have to hold together your thighs until someone deserves what's between them

People will always try to tell you how your dreams are not achievable. But what is more important, their beliefs or yours?

Your life is important. You mean something.
You are valuable.

-in case you forgot

Let that shit go. Let that person go. Let that situation go.

-just let go

They might look better, dress better, and
leave you stress free.

*-but no one can replace the person you
really connected with*

Your desire to rise
must be greater than
their desire to see you fall.

Each day of progress prepares you for
fulfilling your goals

-*work on your goals each day*

You have to be strong enough to walk away from situations that are toxic so that each person may grow, prosper, and see things more clearly.

-that includes family, lovers, and friends

You have a voice. You have a purpose, a reason. Do not let any negativity this world brings you stop you from seeing that.

Never let them see you with tears spilling out
your eyes

-*They don't deserve to see you cry*

For dreams are just dreams if they go untouched

-Turn your dreams into goals

Stop comparing your life to others. Someone else's grass may seem greener but have you taken the time to really water your own?

I hope today you find a purpose to keep going. I hope you don't let yesterday consume the pieces of your tomorrow

What are you
doing with your time?

To be honest, if I didn't have writing I don't know where I would be. It was the first piece of peace I knew. For so long I've dreamed of publishing a book and I finally found the strength to share the parts of me I had kept hidden for so long. *Pieces* was my chance to finally break-free from my chains through a collection of short poems, quotes, and those late night thoughts that seem to find their way through the cracks at the wee hours of the night. I wanted to let you know that you are not alone. Sometimes it's hard talking to other people about what you are going through. *Pieces* is a way of connecting when all signals seem lost. It's a way of talking when there is no one to truly listen.

Writing this book helped reveal some dark thoughts and ugly truths that needed to be to faced. Sometimes we're afraid to be ourselves. But I've decided to peel off the mask I'd conditioned myself to wear. We can't be afraid to live our truths, to live outside the lines, and take our own roads. We were each given our own mind, body and soul. It's what drives us. It's what makes each of us who we are. But it is that same energy that pulls us together.

In our darkest times we don't find the light, we create it. We have to keep spreading unity, peace, love, and wisdom. We have to become that positive energy, that higher frequency, and elevate above our situations. At times when I was writing *Pieces* I was in a dark space. But, I had to be above the water. We have to pull ourselves up when we are sinking. This is a message to say that we will get through our darkest times. The times I wanted to give up, I picked up my pen and found some peace. You have to keep going, keep chasing after whatever makes you happy. No matter what your goals are, go after them. Don't ever give up on yourself. People will always say how you *can't* do something. Fuck the people who don't believe in you. I believe in you. You have to believe too. No matter what you are going through you will bounce back. Believe that.

My story is just a piece of the puzzle, together we are whole. All of our stories mean something. Together we can blossom, together we can change.

I just truly want to thank you. Thank you for taking this journey with me. Thank you for inspiring me. Thank you for taking the time to experience these words and giving me the chance to share pieces of me with you. Through everything this life has tossed me, all I've had was my dreams. I had been told countless times that my dreams were silly and really of no value. But here we are. Thank you for being a part of making them come true. That means more than you could ever know.

Thank you for taking this journey with me

First and foremost, I want to thank you, Mom. You've *always* believed in me. There is no amount of words to express my gratitude. You are why I keep pushing and going. Thank you for pushing me, showing me I am worthy when I felt worthless. Thank you for being my backbone, my number one supporter and helping me find my way through this crazy thing we call life. I am truly blessed to have you. You are more than my mother. You are my world. I can't wait until the day I can at least repay you for even half of the things you have done for me. Just know I am going to keep my promises. *I love you, always.*

Thank you to all my beautiful friends and family who have always supported me and inspired me to let my words fly free. Thank you to the universe. For I appreciate all the experiences I have faced. Without those lessons I am nothing. Thank you for the most beautiful love I have ever encountered. For it has sparked a blazing fire within me.

Thank you

Email: aliyahsouder@gmail.com
Instagram: _aliyahbranay